Motivating
To Win!

How to Create, Inspire and Motivate a High Performing Team.

The story of what happened when the business coach became a sports coach!

David Clark

British Library Cataloguing In Publication Data
A Record of this Publication is available
from the British Library

ISBN 1846854237
978-1-84685-423-1

First Published 2006 by

Exposure Publishing,
an imprint of Diggory Press,
Three Rivers, Minions, Liskeard,
Cornwall, PL14 5LE, UK
WWW.DIGGORYPRESS.COM

This book is dedicated to:

Angela, for all her support and the editing.

Tim, Seb, and Ameisha, for putting up with my obsession!

Floyd Barnett for his help, advice, guidance, support and, above all else, patience!

The Wadebridge Camels under 13 Rugby Team of the 2005/2006 Season, forever remembered as:

"The Titans"

Good Luck for the future!

You know who you are:

Aaron, Aiden, Andy, Ayden, Ben, Ben, Dan, Henry, George, Jack, Jake, James, Liam, Luke, Matt, Merlin, Mike, Mike, Patrick, Ozzy, Richard, Seb, Tom, Tom, Sam,

About the Author

David Clark is a performance coach. He works with individuals, teams and leaders from the world of business to help them improve their performance. His areas of specialism include motivation, personal effectiveness, teambuilding and leadership.

He is originally from Zimbabwe, where he was born and educated, and where he was actively involved in rugby, basketball and water-polo.

In 1973, following the completion of his National Service, David travelled to the U.K. where he has lived ever since.

Involved with people development since the early eighties, he has been running his own consultancy since 1991.

In September 2002 he returned to rugby as a keen parent, after a 30 year gap and is currently a Level 2 Coach and Level 1 Referee.

David lives in Cornwall with his wife Angela and three of his five children.

How to use this book

As you read through the book you will come across ideas or trigger some of your own. Whichever they are, always have a pen with you and write them down.

Write them in the margins, use a highlighter, do whatever you have to in order to make a record of them. The best ideas are sometimes the first ones to hit you, like a flash of the blindingly obvious. However, fast as they come, so they go – so record them.

This should be used as your work book – forget what you were told about not writing notes in margins – just do it.

Then do something about them – take action or, as my friend M.J.A continually told me, quick as a flash, nothing happens.

Chapters

Whatever you can do, or
dream you can do, begin
it.

Boldness has genius, power
and magic in it.

Goethe

In the Beginning.

The world is full of high performing teams. In remote parts of the globe, tribal hunters, seeking food for their families, operate in teams and without teamwork would not survive.

In the animal kingdom there are lots of examples of high performance teams – from wolves in the Tundra to lions hunting on the plains of Africa.

And, in the civilised world, high performing teams exist in abundance, particularly in the areas of business and sport.

Success in the extremely competitive world of business is achieved through teamwork. Large organisations usually consist of a series of teams and sub teams, each of them specialist in their own right, whose performances combine to deliver results.

These teams and sub teams are usually co-ordinated by a top team who harness the individual efforts and successes and convert them into corporate performance.

Business is very competitive, at a number of levels, and in attempting to develop winning approaches, a vast amount of money, time and resource has been invested in finding

If I have seen further
than others, it is by
standing on the shoulders
of giants.

Isaac Newton

ways to maximise performance and results through the development of knowledge, skills and the motivation of the most valuable resource there is – people.

Commonly known as "people development", there are four core areas in which development takes place. These are identified as:

- People development
- Team development
- Leadership development
- Organisational development.

There has been, and still is, a tremendous amount of research carried out by a great number of organisational and behavioural psychologists as well as academics on an international basis to try and find ways to maximise performance, and subsequently results, in all four core areas.

This has lead to the creation of numerous theories, principles and models that have been and indeed are being used in the exciting and demanding world of business today, to create and maintain high performing teams, whose aim is to produce outstanding results.

By way of brief explanation the difference between theories, principles and models is this:

- A theory suggests that if you carry out certain actions you may obtain a particular result.

- A principle is a concrete approach backed up by historic evidence.

- A model demonstrates the stages to be followed in either a theoretical approach to a situation, or the application of a principle.

In the world of business, these are used to great effect, and where they have been introduced, there can be little dispute over their effectiveness.

However I was interested in exploring what effect they could have in a demanding and competitive sporting environment.

Historically, there has been a cross-over from the sports world and the world of adventure to the business world.

Current and past sportsmen and women, together with adventurers have created a whole industry in corporate entertaining and book writing, relating their own personal experiences and offering their thoughts on how to improve teamwork and leadership in the workplace.

However, as far as I could discover, no-one appeared to have made the journey in the opposite direction, to explore whether the techniques used in the creation of high performing business teams could be used with success in the world of sport.

What I was interested in was whether the theories, principles and models used in the corporate environment could be used to great effect in the world of sports.

What would happen if they were applied in the sports world?

Are there similarities between building a high performing team in the workplace and building a high performing team in the sports environment?

There was also another thing. One of the challenges in working in the area of people development is that invariably as an external consultant, my involvement is fairly limited.

I am commissioned to design and deliver a development event and once run my involvement is then over. I am not normally around to see what results are created when

A good objective of
leadership is to help those
who are doing poorly to do
well, and to help those
who are doing well to do
even better.

Jim Rohn

the learning from the event is implemented back in the workplace.

What I wanted was to have the opportunity to test out these theories, principles and models in the sports environment and be able to monitor their effectiveness.

In the business world it is generally acknowledged that the most important thing of all is performance, because if you get the performance right, you will do well.

Performance is a by-product of three things, namely knowledge, skill and motivation.

When the performance is right, then success will happen. Of course it is possible to perform well and still come second, but it is unusual to perform poorly and come first.

The key is in developing and managing the level and quality of performance achieved by the team.

Again, in the business world this becomes the responsibility of the leader, and is the sole purpose of leadership.

Ultimately, the level of performance achieved by any team is a reflection of the quality of leadership being supplied.

High performance does not just happen, certainly not in a timely manner.

To be effective in leading, leaders need to be able to develop and grow themselves, as well as being able to grow and develop individuals and teams.

Leaders need to be able to create and improve team performance, and then to maintain it at a high level.

I have been involved in people development for over 20 years, since the early 1980's. My experiences have lead me to work with leaders, teams and individuals in both the public and private sectors, and very interesting experiences they have been too.

Over this time I have worked extensively with a broad range of theories, principles and models and gained a lot of experience with them.

However I was keen to test them out myself in a different environment, partly to check out their validity, and partly for the challenge in making them work.

I was able to do as a result of supporting my two young sons at the rugby club near our home in Cornwall. Over time I gradually became involved in helping their coaches with the coaching, and then one day I became a coach in my own right.

This provided me with the opportunity to see what would happen if the principles, theories and models used in the business world were applied in a sports context.

This is the story of "The Titans".

Officially they were the Wadebridge Camels under-13 side for the 2005-2006 rugby season. Unbeknown to them they became the "guinea pigs" in an experimental project that took place when I as a business coach, became a rugby coach.

It is worth just pointing out that at the time my sons started getting involved in rugby in 2002 I had not been involved with rugby, or indeed any other sport, for around 30 years.

My return to rugby was very interesting to say the least, because by the time I did return, it seemed to me that apart from the number of players on the pitch, and the shape of the ball, everything else was different.

The pitch was measured in metres and the laws and rules had changed to help keep play flowing more. What I could recall was probably more dangerous than what I did not know, so I did not start out terribly well!

Although I did not have a great deal to offer by way of recent rugby playing experience, I did have a lot of belief in myself and my ability to learn.

I believed that I could make a reasonable success of the project, provided of course that the basics of building a high performance team were the same in both business and sport.

Time would tell.

*Your legacy should be
that you made it better
than it was when you got
it*

Lee Iacoca

High Performing Teams.

What is a high performing team and how does it differ from any other team?

There are some major differences that separate a high performing team from an ordinary one, and surprisingly enough it is not necessarily because the team members are the best there are.

Certainly, top quality team members can make a difference, but ordinary team members can become star performers in a positive team environment.

However, there are some other factors that come into play when high performing teams are created.

The first of these is about how the team performs as a team. High Performing Teams all have certain identifiable characteristics in common. These include:

1) The atmosphere within the team, including between the leader and members of the team, tends to be very informal and relaxed.

2) Everyone is involved in discussions, and their views and opinions are acknowledged although not necessarily agreed with.

3) Everyone is clear about the objective of the team, and personally committed to do all they can to achieve it.

4) There are openness, honesty and high levels of trust within the team, and between the members of the team and the leader.

5) It is safe to voice disagreement and members feel comfortable in doing so, demonstrating willingness to voice opinions and discuss them.

6) No single individual seeks to dominate the others – there is a democratic approach to issues

7) There are agreed decision making procedures which everyone has signed up to before they are needed

8) Feedback between members to members is regular, frank and honest, and intended to help improve team performance.

8) The team allocates time to discussing the team and how well it is working, at a process level.

9) Everyone is clear about individual responsibilities, particularly their own.

10) The team is empowered to make relevant decisions and encouraged to take responsibility for doing so where appropriate.

11) The team is totally united behind the cause, and for each other.

12) There is high evidence of teamwork, and teamwork is the mantra.

13) The members of the team deal with internal issues themselves.

14) The members of the team support each other and can call on each other for support.

15) The performance of team members as individuals is greater within the team than it could be as individuals outside the team.

16) Each team member gives 100% of their capability 100% of the time.

However, high performance teams do not come about by accident. They have to be created, developed and maintained, and that is the role of the leader.

Individuals play the games, but teams beat the odds.

U.S. Navy Seals

High Performing Leaders.

Ultimately, leadership is about producing results, and the way in which leaders set out to achieve these results is through the performance of the team.

Therefore, the more effective the leadership is, the better the team performance will be.

To be effective in achieving results, a leader has to be able to demonstrate competency in three core areas.

These are the ability to direct the team and the individual members, the ability to motivate the team and the members of it, and finally the ability to deal with issues of non-compliance or underperformance in an assertive manner.

Effective leadership therefore requires three core abilities, namely the ability to direct, motivate and be assertive.

The first thing a leader needs to do is to provide direction to the team and each individual member of the team.

Direction covers a number of things, including specific instruction, creating a vision and providing guidance.

Direction gives a purpose or focus to the efforts of the team, something to aim for or at.

Motivation is about inspiring individuals to put in the maximum effort they can, to become the best they can, and to trigger their self motivation.

It releases an inner energy or force, and good leaders always seek to access this energy so that it can be harnessed and used to good effect. It is the harnessing of energy that enables the potential to be harvested.

Without motivation, potential remains just that – potential. Leadership is concerned with getting the best and the most from people and helping them to convert their potential into performance.

 Inspirational leadership captures the hearts and minds of those people and creates a strong commitment to "the cause". An inspirational leader provides the team with a vision of what can be, and encourages the team to achieve it, raising individual and team performance on the way.

The third core ability is assertiveness.
In the context of leadership, assertiveness defines the leader's willingness to deal with

First say to yourself what
you would be, and then do
what you have to do.

Epictetus

issues, particularly with aspects of non-performance or non-compliance, as and when they arise.

Lack of willingness to deal with difficult situations or people is interpreted as a sign of weak leadership and can set off a chain of events that leads to low morale, lowered motivation and variable commitment. This is in fact everything that effective leadership is not about.

However, there is more to leadership than just being competent in these three areas.

The effectiveness of leadership is a by-product of how it is delivered, and the most effective way to deliver leadership in the medium to long term, in order to maintain high levels of morale and motivation, is via positive influence.

Leadership also involves influence, and everything a leader says, or does, has the capacity to exert either a positive or a negative influence.

Over the years of working with leaders I have identified five distinct levels of leadership influence and have put these together in a model which I have named "The Pentado Model of Leadership Influence".

This model incorporates all the main leadership and motivational theories, principles and models into one leadership model, and it was this model that was to become the mainstay of what I came to know as "The Titans' Project."

The Pentado model asserts that to be effective as a leader, an individual has to be effective at five separate levels as follows:

- "I" Centred Leadership
- "People" Centred Leadership
- "Team" Centred Leadership
- "Performance" Centred Leadership
- "Transformation" Centred Leadership.

Each of these levels deals with a particular component of leadership effectiveness, and is sometimes referred to as being an "inside – out" model.

This type of model begins with the individual themselves, and moves up through different environments.

So, for example, the first level deals with what goes on within the leader and how they manage themselves.

Level two looks at relating to others.

The third level deals with working with groups, whilst the fourth level deals with a more traditional approach to leading groups.

The last level deals with transformation and change, to deal with changing environments and circumstances.

Leaders need to be aware that their influence at all five levels has a significant impact on the morale and motivation of the team members and for this reason alone need to be self aware in order to ensure that they exert a positive influence at all times.

Many individuals with great leadership potential undermine their personal effectiveness by underestimating this fact, and consequently find themselves leading an under performing team.

Each of these levels is important in their own right, and leaders need to understand each level and the impact the influence will have on the members of the team, either positively or negatively.

Level 1 - "I Centred Leadership"

This level is concerned with the leader as an individual, and their personal ability to deal with a range of situations.

These include their ability to set personal and business goals, their personal organisation, personal learning, problem solving and decision making skills and their ability to cope with pressure.

It also includes their self awareness, which involves their ability to understand both themselves and what effect their behaviour can and does have on others.

Leadership is transparent – every action carried out by the leader is visible, and has an impact on the minds of others. Whilst leaders do not have to be perfect in everything they do, it certainly helps their cause if the balance of successes swings in their favour.

A leader has to model what he or she is looking for in the team members, and act as role models.

If a leader is to have credibility and have the respect of team members then they have to be seen to be doing things well. Team members will have great personal difficulty in believing in and respecting someone who, for example is totally disorganised, forgets important appointments or is always beset with problems and unresolved issues.

They will find it hard to show respect for and to someone if the behaviour of that person does not command respect in the first place.

When I was first elected to the role of team coach, I set out certain things that I wanted to achieve.

The long term goal was to be in a position to compete for and hopefully win the knockout competition at the end of two years. There were numerous shorter term goals.

One was to obtain sponsorship for training equipment, shirts and training suits.

Another was to develop a regular routine of contacting the players every Friday evening or Saturday morning in order to confirm their availability, directions to the match etc., so that there would be no surprises on the day.

This meant having to organise myself and the other demands that there were on my time so that these tasks which I also considered to be important, could be carried out.

I was also very aware of my own level of competence, or incompetence, depending upon whether you see the glass half full or half empty.

I felt that as a coach I owed it to the young players that I was responsible for, to see that they got the best coaching that I could provide for them.

That meant two things to me. One was that as far as my personal learning was concerned, I had to accelerate it.

I had to develop a greater knowledge base and skill set.

That meant reading, attending courses, watching games, videos and DVD's, observing and talking to other coaches and gaining as much personal experience, feedback and coaching as I could.

The other thing was to find people who could help me to fill the knowledge and skills gap, whilst I went through the learning process.

That was done by enlisting the help of parents who had played rugby before, and who had a good knowledge of the game.

By building a coaching team I was able to create the knowledge and skill base needed, although no one individual person had all of it themself, including me.

Level 2 - "People Centred Leadership".

This level of leadership influence is concerned with building strong and healthy relationships with people.

It is not necessarily about getting people to like you, but it is concerned with the giving and receiving of respect.

Skill and knowledge at this level centre on personal communication skills, which include basic interpersonal skills, negotiation skills, influencing skills and assertiveness.

The ability to manage a range of inter-personal situations is very important and the effective leader needs to develop a range of skills to be able to do so.

The skills can be used within the team and also in terms of dealing with situations that are external to the team.
Apart from anything else, leaders need to be able to demonstrate common courtesy to people, and expect the same in return. There should be little if any reason that dignity and grace cannot be maintained by the leader at all times, and encouraged in others.

In order to achieve the goals I had for the team, I knew that I needed to build good relationships with the players, my fellow coaches, and players parents.

I needed the players' commitment and that of the other parties involved so that I could depend upon their attendance. I also wanted to get to know more about everyone as individuals which would be very important when it came to motivation.

However, it was also important that everyone understood what any necessary rules were, and what was expected of them in terms of their behaviour and performance, and it was important for me to make sure everyone had a good grasp of what was what.

For example, players were not to expect to be allowed to miss a training session without good reason, and then to turn up on Sunday for a match and be part of the starting line up, providing of course we had sufficient players. Similarly, they needed to understand what was acceptable and unacceptable on the field of play – bad behaviour and attitude was not going to be tolerated.

Not only is leadership transparent, it also needs to be consistent. Good leadership is required at all times, through both the good and the bad times.

To climb steep hills
requires a slow pace at
first.

Shakespeare

Leaders need to deal with people in a consistent manner so that those being lead know where they stand.

It requires both honesty and integrity at all times. "Fair weather" leadership, only getting involved when things go well, does not work. It does not provide the support and guidance required to deal with difficult times and issues, and leads to high levels of dissatisfaction.

This level of the leadership model has to be worked at quite hard by some of us, and is no place for the weak hearted.

Level 3 - "Team Centred Leadership".

This level of the leadership model is concerned with converting the raw materials or building blocks of the team, the individuals themselves, into the team itself.

It requires leaders to have developed a good understanding of the individual and team motivation, as well as all the processes involved in the formation of a team.

In particular they need to understand the challenges and barriers that exist which can and do impede the development of the team.

Interestingly, the more motivated and highly developed the individuals become, the greater the potential challenge for the leader.

The role of the leader becomes one of inspiring motivation in the individuals and then harnessing the energy this creates to form the team.

There has been a lot of work carried out in the area of both personal and workplace motivation.

The two most popular modern theories on these topics are written up in the separate research carried out by Abraham Maslow and Frederick Herzberg.

Not only are they the most popular and well known, but they are also tried and tested and they are known to work.

Young players come along to rugby for a number of reasons. According to the work of Maslow, if they are at rugby voluntarily, it will probably be for one of three reasons.

Firstly, they want to be with like-minded people and belong to the rugby scene.

There is probably something within the rugby camaraderie that appeals to them, which might be a simple as being with friends or belonging to a rugby team.

The second reason could be for some sort of social cachet – the prestige of being acknowledged as being a rugby player, and the perceived status attached to that.

Finally, according to Maslow's research, a small minority of players will be present at rugby because they simply want to be the best rugby players that they can be, to suit themselves.

However there is one other significant reason why young players turn up at rugby.

That is because some significant adult has decided it will be good for them, possibly having them follow in the footsteps of a father or older brother.

Not all members of this group particularly want to be at rugby, but feel they have no alternative and would rather attend something they would prefer not to, as opposed to letting someone down or facing their wrath or disappointment.

From a coaches perspective I felt very sorry for the members of the last group. They were like square pegs in a round hole and you could tell from their overall demeanour and body language that their hearts were not in rugby.

I felt that the best way forward with these young players was to try and motivate and develop them in the hope that they would become converts to the game, and end up enjoying it.

Taking into account the very physical nature of the game, it is not really a place for the faint hearted, and can actually make it more dangerous for them due to their lack of commitment.

There are parallels with the workplace however, in terms of the occasional individual who for whatever reason finds themselves trapped in a job they do not

Great spirits have always
encountered opposition
from mediocre minds.

Albert Einstein

really enjoy, but need to attend in order to earn a living.

Again, from a coaching or leadership perspective, it is much easier to work with the willing as there is less overall resistance.

Whereas Maslow sought to explain individual's motivation and the behavioural drivers behind it, Frederick Herzberg was looking at motivation in the workplace and which particular actions or aspects actually had a positive impact on personal motivation and therefore performance.

Herzberg identified 5 actions that could be taken in the workplace by managers and leaders that were the keys to triggering workplace motivation.

He said that one of these was the job, or activity itself, which people became involved with because it had a motivational effect on them.

In simple terms, people are motivated by being involved in that which they enjoy.

The second key was achievement, or the opportunity to achieve.

Herzberg identified that people like a challenge that holds out the possibility of achieving something positive.

The third key was defined as advancement, which includes both personal and skill development. If individuals are growing as people and through their skill development are improving their performance then there is a motivational effect attached.

Fourth on the list comes responsibility.

Individuals respond well to being given the right level of responsibility. Insufficient can be demeaning, and too much of it can be frightening.

However, giving someone the appropriate level of responsibility will motivate them and improve their performance.

Finally Herzberg identified probably the most powerful motivator of them all – personal recognition.

He discovered that individuals at all levels in life enjoy recognition, so much so that they will actually work at obtaining more.

It is addictive and has a tremendous motivational capacity.

One of the things that I believe makes both Maslow's and Herzberg's theories so fascinating and intriguing is the way they compliment each other and almost form a symbiotic relationship.

This information in the hands of a business leader or coach, interested in improving performance, is absolute dynamite – if they recognise it.

In simple terms, an individual seeking to be included as part of a team, to satisfy their need to belong, can have their personal performance levels enhanced through a series of challenging development activities that are accompanied by genuine praise and recognition.

The encouragement will enable them to strive to gain more by working harder, thus increasing their personal abilities and the contribution they make to the team.

This might seem like an oversimplification, believe me it isn't.

To be able to be accepted into the team, individuals have to make a contribution, or be able to make a contribution, to team success.

The better able to do this they are, the quicker that acceptance and inclusion will happen.

Those with a leadership role can use this type of approach to improve individual and team performance, although they will often have to work at it in order to create appropriate opportunities.

Whilst the development of the team is in progress, the leader has to be continuously questioning the effectiveness of their personal actions.

They should at least be asking themselves:

- Am I making the experience of being here as enjoyable as possible?

- Am I setting the right level of challenge, or managing high levels of challenge appropriately?

- Am I finding opportunities to provide good honest feedback and positive recognition?

- Am I giving responsibility to people wherever I can?

- Are the individuals developing and advancing their knowledge and skills?

They should probably also be asking themselves:

- Are they enjoying themselves?

- Are they developing / improving?

- Are they demonstrating / displaying teamwork and co-operation?

- What else do I need to do to facilitate the creation of the team?

and anything else they can think of.

My experience of working with leaders is that all too often a high percentage of them are not really prepared to put in the effort required to be effective leaders and motivators.

Unfortunately they seem to pay lip service to the matter of motivation in particular, either considering it beneath them, or just not bothered about it.

Like all things in life, some of us find certain things come more naturally than others.

*If you are not going all
the way, why go at all?*

Joe Namath

Some individuals seem to be able to do things in an apparently effortless fashion.

Whichever applies, effective leadership requires certain actions to be taken whether it requires a lot of effort or not on the part of the leader.

The secret to high motivation seems to me to be a case of continuously looking out for opportunities to give even small amounts of praise and recognition, knowing how powerful a motivator it is.

Where possible, I would urge leaders to try and create opportunities for success to be achieved, through which positive feedback can be provided.

Positive feedback can be used to leverage further improvements in performance, thus bringing about further opportunities for feedback.

Once the cycle is set up, it is possible to use it to drive performance upwards.

Effective leadership does not come about by accident. It has to be worked at, and continuously.

The leader is always in a position to influence, and needs to manage the process of influence.

However, highly motivated and skilled individuals do not automatically move towards becoming a team.

The team has to be created. Also, a group is not the same as a team. You can take a group of rugby players and put them on a pitch, but they will not play as well as a well formed team.

The first stage on the journey is to have the ability to recognise the difference between a team and a group.

There is a significant difference, and both require different leadership approaches.

A group is a collection of individuals who may all be very highly skilled, but who are more concerned with achieving their own goals at an individual level, than co-operating with others to achieve a common goal.

A team on the other hand, is a collection of individuals who have come together to co-operate in the attempt to meet a goal that is common to them as a team. In doing so, they may have put their own goals to one side, even temporarily.

In practice however, team-players invariably can get their own needs and goals met by contributing to the success of the team.

To build a team, the leader is essentially turning a group of individuals into a cohesive unit.

The transition from group to team has five identifiable stages, each of which requires a different approach.

Based on the original work of Bruce Tuckman, these stages are identified as:

- Formation

- Stagnation

- Divination

- Creation

- Reformation

Formation.

This is the early stages when the individuals are first brought together and their expectations and enthusiasm are high. It is also a time when there can be a lot of personal posturing and pouting! There is a lot of energy, mostly misguided and un-harnessed.

This stage normally requires a lot of leader input, often in a directive style. It can be a very testing time for the new leader.

Your chances of success in
any undertaking can
always be measured by
your belief in yourself.

Robert Collier

Stagnation.

The posturing increases as individuals compete for status and recognition, completely losing sight of what they are there to do in some cases. The tension increases, teddy bears are thrown out of prams and dummies are spat out.

There can be a lot of uncertainty. People are unaware of their roles and the roles of others and it can feel like fighting for personal survival.

The leaders' role will never seem less pleasurable. When a group are at this stage it requires a very high investment of energy from the leader to try and maintain direction and prevent the group from fragmenting further, possibly disintegrating.

Divination

When the team is in the Stagnation phase, the only way to move forward is for the leader to create a divination phase. This is a phase where the group and the leader, discuss what is going on within the group, and what needs to happen in order for the group to undergo a transition and to become a team.

Whilst facilitated by the leader, it is up to the individuals in the group to take responsibility for bringing about the change from group to team. This involves agreeing rules and procedures that they all abide by. Individual roles and responsibilities are defined and understood, and the group starts to operate more like a team.

It is relatively easy to throw a group of individuals together and experience stages one and two. However, unless the whole process is managed well, level three will not be reached, resulting in a very poorly performing group.

It is normally this stage that teambuilding events are set up to deal with, enabling the transition to the next phase.

Creation.

Level four is defined as Creation. The team is still in it's infancy, but with the new found structure, processes etc it can start to practice teamwork, with the increased performance this brings. The leader is now more like a person with a hand on the tiller of a boat, with the team acting as the dynamic powerhouse that drives the boat forward.

The leader has to monitor and adjust performance, but by now it is more about fine tuning than anything else. The role of the leader moves from creating and building a team to maintaining the team, occasionally having to step in and deal with major issues that arise from time to time.

Quite often during the transition from Divination to Creation, a team will create its own team identity, separate to the official identity. This is where the team members show most loyalty and allegiance.

They can because they
think they can.

Virgil

Reformation.

The final level is reformation, which is very similar to the first level, formation. When a team changes, either by the addition or departure of an individual, it is no longer the same team. It is a new team and the process begins again. This is one area where work and sports teams differ significantly.

A work team is usually a lean team, with no spare capacity or people, whereas a sports team will have a number of substitutes available. For those substitutes to be effective, they must not only understand the responsibilities of the role they are going to fulfil, but they must also understand the team tactics and strategies, and how they fit in to them. When a substitute goes onto the field of play they must be able to fit into the team as if they were part of the original team, and contribute as well or better than the person they have replaced.

Inexperienced leaders, particularly in the workplace fail to recognise this stage, and

do not understand how what seems to be a comparatively simple change can have such a big effect.

One version of this model includes in this stage an effect called mourning, which bewilders managers completely at times. The effect of someone leaving the team does more than simply change the structure of the team. It can also mean the loss of a tried and trusted friend, and those remaining can enter a period of mourning for the loss of the friend.

Leaders generally fail to recognise and understand this, and in their misguided efforts to get things "back to normal" can actually do more damage than they realise to morale and motivation.

In summary, teamwork does not happen by accident – it has to be worked at. The role of the leader at this level is to ensure that the raw materials or building blocks, which are the individuals who will make up the team, are motivated to a high degree, and then facilitate the transition from group to team.

Once the team is formed and performing the role of the leader switches to team maintenance, in order to ensure that the highest possible levels of performance are achieved and maintained.

Talent wins games, but
teamwork and
intelligence wins
championships.

Magic Johnson

Level 4 - Performance Centred Leadership.

This level in the Pentado Hierarchy deals with performance, and doing what is required to bring about high performance.

Performance is a by-product of three factors:

- Motivation

- Knowledge

- Skills

Having already looked at motivation, we now turn our attention to the other two.

Knowledge and skills are covered through 5 separate areas.

These are:

- Goals

- Guidelines

- Communication

- Development Activities

- Culture of Performance.

The first thing everyone in the team needs to be aware of is lumped under the generic title of goals.

This includes the goals of the leader for the team, the performance targets for the team, standards to be met, individual's goals, and any key performance measures that are important.

These give the team a focus for what they do.

Secondly, it is important for the team to know what guidelines they must follow, including health and safety, legal, corporate and process.

It is essential that every member of the team knows the frame work within which they have to operate, to keep themselves and the team "legal".

Number three on the list is communications. The leader of the team has a responsibility to ensure that the team receives whatever information they need, and that they receive it in an appropriate and timely manner.

This includes feedback on both personal and team performance.

The fourth item relates to development activities.

If you as a leader are asking members of the team to perform to a certain standard, then you need to ensure that they have all the knowledge and skills they need to perform to that standard. The development that is required can be decided by observation or through discussion or, in most cases both.

Finally, we come to what I refer to as a culture of performance. In some areas this is referred to as "walking the talk".

It simply means that the leader is prepared to deal with issues in an appropriate and timely manner.

Things are not left to fester or ignored in the hope that they will either improve of their own accord, or disappear.

The leader sets an example of leadership and deals with situations appropriately.

These five sub levels create the route to success through performance.

They also provide the mechanism to enable the monitoring of performance and, through development actions, bring about any necessary improvement.

Level 5 - Transformation Centred Leadership

The final level in the Pentado Model deals with change, also known as transformation.

Nothing stays the same for long, not people, not circumstances, nor job roles. An effective leader firstly has to be able to manage themself as situations and circumstances demand, and bring about the required transition. This will normally involve an element of learning, and application of that learning.

The leader also has to be able to manage the individuals and the team through transformation, to meet the rapidly changing demands being faced every day.

Finally, the leader must be capable of setting time aside to review performance past and future, to ensure that it is always equal to the

demands placed upon the team, and the leader themselves.

Effective leadership in the workplace can be achieved through the Pentado Model of Leadership Influence, but the big question that I wanted to answer was could it be used to good effect in the sports environment, and if so, how far could it take a team.

Whatever you can do, or
dream you can do, begin
it.

Boldness has genius, power
and magic in it.

Goethe

The Titans Project – How it all began

In September 2004 when the rugby season began, I was a coach without a team.

I stood for election at the end of the previous season as coach for the under 15's. I wanted to move up with them and their original coach had decided to move on, however, the club decided to bring in a new coach so that left me "team less".

Whilst my older son was now an under 15, my youngest son decided that he would like to take up club rugby and became a member of the under 12 squad.

I hung around like a spare part, assisting other coaches if they wanted help and I refereed a couple of games.

I also arranged to complete the assessment for my Level 1 coaching qualification along with my friend Paul.

Sundays alternated between watching under 15's and under 12's and helping out. Then it came to light that the person looking after the 12's was about to leave for Portugal, and they were going to be without a coach.

I asked if I could take them on as caretaker and that proved acceptable, so towards the end of October I became the under 12's coach.

What I took on was a real challenge.

At this age group, a team consists of 12 players on the pitch, plus substitutes if there are any.

The team plays on an area which is just under half the size of a normal rugby pitch. The game is played for 20 minutes each way, and uses a size 3 ball, which is quite small compared to a normal sized rugby ball.

There are also a number of rules which are different to full blown adult rugby, and which are there for safety reasons.

What I now discovered I had was slightly different in some respects.

Firstly, we did not have enough players to make up a full team, never mind substitutes. That meant that whenever we turned up to play a game we had to borrow players from our opposition, not the best way to field a cohesive team!

Secondly, the skill level of the players was pretty poor.

We had players that did not care in which direction they ran or in which direction they passed the ball, or who they passed it to! Very useful to the opposition, that was!

Thirdly, in terms of commitment to the team, rugby was something some of them did if there was nothing better to do.

If Gran was cooking a roast lunch, they were not at rugby!

The other issue as I previously eluded to was the reason for being there at all. Most had at least a vague interest in rugby, but some were there to satisfy the needs of others.

However, whatever the reason, they were all that I had.

I quickly recognised that there were certain steps that had to be taken in the short term, in order to improve the situation drastically for the better.

Firstly, I had to recruit new players to the squad, and quickly.

This was critical if I was going to have any chance of creating a team of any description.

Eagles don't flock. You
have to find them one at
a time.

H. Ross Perot

Secondly, there was a need to develop the most basic of skill levels in order to create a platform for long term skill development.

Until we got the basic skills right, there was no point in even thinking about some of the more advanced skills and tactics.

Finally, there was motivation.

I wanted to build up player motivation – I wanted and needed every single individual to turn up to training and matches on every occasion, if necessary going to Gran's lunch afterwards – the roasters could wait!

There was more to it than that though.

I felt that the best source of new players was the existing squad. If they went to school and raved about rugby in an enthusiastic manner, then there was every chance that they would attract some of their school friends, and that was important to our long term success.

Not only that, but when new recruits turned up, I wanted them to want to come back.

I decided I needed to make a three pronged approach to start with that would include:

- Making training enjoyable.

- Developing knowledge and skills within myself and the payers.

- Gain the commitment of parents and players to the team.

That required a number of deliberate actions.

Firstly sessions had to be planned around the needs of the individuals and the team.

The content of those sessions had to combine the development of individual, unit and team skills, as well as have time for a game of rugby at the end.

The reason most of the lads (for they were all lads) came to rugby was to play it.

So much so that the time spent on the development of skills was largely seen by the team as unnecessary by them to begin with.

This changed as they realised that other teams were ahead of them in terms of their own development, and that was why they were finding it hard to win.

However, by combining fun and personal challenge in the training we got through a lot of work, and they could see themselves developing and improving.

During this time I was looking for examples of good practice or good performance that would enable me to provide praise and recognition to every player concerned.

It did not matter how small an achievement it was, and it was invariably accompanied by some advice or guidance on how they could improve further, in quite small, achievable increments.

I produced an address book of names and phone numbers, including the names of parents and brothers and sisters

Every week, normally on a Friday evening, I would phone everyone up to make sure they would be available for training or for the match on the Sunday.

Whoever answered the phone, I wanted them to be able to use their name when talking to them. I wanted them to feel valued, because they were.

They were part of the wider team, the supporters and followers, who I considered a very important group of people.

They not only supported the team, they also helped to make my life easier.

The regular phoning also gave me a chance to talk to the parents. I used the opportunity to find out how they thought their sons were getting on at rugby and whether they were enjoying it.

This gave me an insight into how the young player was feeling towards the way I was running things, and allowed me to deal with anything that I felt necessary.

All players were asked if they knew anyone at school or elsewhere that could play rugby, and were encouraged to ask them to come along.

At the same time I offered my services to local schools to provide coaching and refereeing services in order to get the chance to meet more potential squad members.

And it started to work.

During the remainder of that season we saw our numbers go from less than twelve to finish the season with 22.

Some of those players had ability and potential, and some didn't. That did not matter.
They were part of the squad, and welcomed accordingly. Slower developers simply take

longer to get there – I should know as I am one!

Of course, as the numbers grew it became harder to manage the sessions so it was time to enlist help.

This came in the traditional way – parents who stood on the sidelines watching, and who were prepared to get involved. Soon we had a team of four or five of us who turned out regularly to help develop the squad.

I introduced a "Man of The Match" trophy, to be awarded every week to the player who was deemed to have made the biggest contribution to teamwork during a game.

I believe very strongly in the principle that you get what you reward, and teamwork was essential to high performance and ultimate success.

One of my biggest successes was creating a website for the team, which included all our fixtures, brief match reports and a "rogue's gallery" of photographs of the players (all with permission gained from the players and their parents) and coaches.

I praise loudly – I blame softly.

Catherine the Great.

There was also a man of the match page
with a photograph of the winner.

The site received a huge amount of hits every week, with occasional emails being sent from various school computers asking me what I was up to, had I found any lost property etc. It really proved very popular with all the players.

It also played a very important part in communication as I could put directions to away fixtures there which got parents involved as well. It turned out to be much more successful than I had ever envisaged.

We got through the rest of the season with a few victories under our belts against the sides that had beaten us earlier on, and we made good progress.

We also went on a short tour to Devon, where a good time was had by all.

At the end of that season I was delighted to be elected coach for the following season, the 2005/6 season, and, as part of my own development I enrolled for a Level 2 coaching course.

I had been investing a lot of time and efforts in my personal development, and felt this would have a significant impact. It did.

Do not follow where the path may lead. Go instead where there is no path and leave one for others to follow.

Ralph Waldo Emerson

The New Season

Prior to the start of the new season I sat and thought about what might be.

We had finished the season well, and were improving in all areas all the time. Mind you, so were our opposition.

I believed that if we took a two year approach to team development then with the players I had, and the development that could be provided, there was no reason why, by the end of the second year, we could not be the top team in the county in our age group.

I felt that the target for the end of the approaching season should be to beat all our year group contemporaries.

This would mean that in the following year we could go on developing so that we could compete against the top three with a view to beating them.

At this point, based on my level of experience, I thought it would probably be time to hand the team on to someone with more coaching experience.

However, that did not take into account that over the next two years I would continue to develop myself, so we would have to wait and see.

The season began as always on the first week of September.

Everyone turned up and we began our new season well. This year, as under 13's there were several major changes to the way the team played.

Firstly, they played as a full 15 man side for the first time.

Secondly, they played on the full sized pitch.

Thirdly the game now consisted of 2 halves of 25 minutes each. Therefore there was a greater requirement for both fitness and stamina.

However, we now trained on Wednesday nights and played games on a Sunday, so there was more time available to get fit.

All these changes had to be accommodated, and like all change, some welcomed it and some resisted it.

As change and leadership could fill a book on its own, for now let me just say that it had to be managed through, particularly as some of the initial enthusiasm shown by the players started to wane as the reality of the changes hit them!

During the new season we were very fortunate to receive a large amount of financial sponsorship.

Mark Evans, Head of H.R. at GSK Coleford, manufacturers and suppliers of Ribena and Lucozade products very kindly provided us with sufficient money to buy a complete set of 20 brand new, top quality shirts, which we had embroidered with the Lucozade Sport logo.

One of the players' relatives provided sponsorship through which we were able to purchase training equipment like running poles, hurdles and speed ladders.

A sponsored training session was held on the beach to raise money for training jackets and trousers, which was a lot of fun, and attracted a lot of attention, leading to more players turning up.

Later in the year we were to receive polo shirts, shorts and socks from more kind sponsors.

In total we raised over £3000.00 of sponsorship money.

I took this to be an investment in the team more than anything else, and used this support to help get over the message about how much I and other people believed in the team and were prepared to support it.

I believe this was an essential contribution to developing a strong sense of self belief for each of the players.

The season started reasonably well. We lost the first few games then started to even the score a bit.

Player numbers continued to rise, reaching 28 at one point.

I hoped we would get to two teams but we never quite made it, and numbers dropped back to 25 by the end of the season.

With the numbers we had it was essential now to carry out some teambuilding activities.

We had a wide range of competencies within the team. It would have been easy to select the strongest players and concentrate on winning.

You cannot teach a man anything. You can only help him to find it within himself.

Galileo Galilei

However, the club has a policy of inclusivity – if people are prepared to come along then they get a chance to play in games.

I believe this is the right approach at the younger ages, as children of this age develop at different rates, and who knows whether today's under performer is tomorrows star?

Nevertheless, develop we did, not always with the full support and blessings of the other members of my coaching team, who I believe would have preferred to adopt the strongest team approach at all times.

More players meant more challenges and more conflict.

It was time to make sure that we had a set of rules in place to deal with issues likely to arise.

I introduced these as I deemed appropriate – things like no playing without training, everyone was important to the team, and probably the least popular one which was everyone had to train for at least two positions and do what they were asked, for the team.

Players were continuously encouraged to think "team" as opposed to "me".

One potential problem facing me was what I call the external coaching factor – ex-rugby playing fathers telling their sons what to do if they ever got hold of the ball, and usually contrary to what was being coached.

In the midst of everything else that was going on, the players continued to receive personal praise and recognition for their own achievements, no matter how small, and encouragement to improve.

As the season progressed, so did the team performance.

There were some quite outstanding displays of rugby played, although we were also well beaten by some of the longer established teams. However, we were moving our way up.

One aspect of the maturing team was the identification of team roles or positions.

With 25 players to choose from, I decided that we had to have maximum flexibility to make choices.

To do this I continued to develop players so they could play in different positions if necessary.

For example, I had seven players who could play at prop if needed, several who could play second row, 2 scrumhalves and so on.

At last I had a developing squad that could accommodate injury, illness and absence and still field a semi decent if not excellent team!

The squad was demonstrating many of the characteristics of a rapidly maturing team.

There was more concern for the team and teamwork than for individuals themselves, which was very gratifying.

The team were very good at recognising the contribution made by individuals and providing genuine congratulations. And the team started to be able to recognise their own performance shortcomings which we then attempted to deal with during training.

All was not perfect however – we still had one or two super-egos, and we still had one or two who talked rugby better than they played.

But now the team were starting to deal with their own issues, so things in these areas started to improve.

And then one day, something quite fascinating happened.

The team captain, a quite outstanding player by the name of Liam, suddenly referred to the team as "The Titans" during one of the pre-match huddles.

Where it came from I do not know, but the name stuck.

From then on the team were known as "The Titans", and the team identity had been created.

One of the key characteristics of a maturing team that is capable of high performance is that the team creates its own identity, and that is what Liam had done.

Overall it had the effect of bonding the players together in a true Cornish "one for all and all for one" approach.

From that moment on, performance seemed to improve significantly.

So much so that we started to beat some of the teams long considered our betters. In fact, we did so well that we ended up in the semi-finals of the knockout cup against one of the strongest under 13 sides in Cornwall.

Never give up. Never,
never give up. You only
begin to fail when you
stop trying to succeed.

Winston S Churchill.

They proved too strong for us in the first half and ran up a big score.

Although we had no chance of beating them, at half time I urged our team to go back out and play as a team and simply enjoy themselves.

They played a completely different game, lots of good rugby, and had no more points scored against them.

There is no doubt the better team won, but the players demonstrated their worth in the second half and next season the teams they face will see a different team when they meet the Titans again.

The season was a good one for the Titans.

They got much further in the first year than was planned.

By the end of the season they had become a very cohesive team, and had a very high skill compared to that which they had when they started.

There is still a lot of work to do, but now there is a solid platform to work from.

The squad finished the year with 25 players, a net gain of 3.

I have no doubt that next year more new players will join – there is nothing like success to attract new blood.

During the season I continued with my own personal development work, attending a coach development programme and qualifying as a Level 2 coach, which has since opened further doors for me.

And what of the future, from autumn 2006 and beyond?

Who knows?

I have taken on a coaching role at a different club, where I am looking forward to the challenge of starting over again, but this time with much more experience.

An opportunity has also arisen to assist in the coaching of youth players within the county development structure. This brings me into contact with very experienced coaches, and I am working with young players that have been identified as having high potential.

All this will be good for my continuing personal development.

During August 2006 I was one of the assistant coaches at a south west England rugby camp, run by a certain England Rugby World Cup captain, which provided a fantastic opportunity to both contribute and learn from others.

I thoroughly enjoyed my time as the Titans coach. They are a great bunch of lads with a good future in rugby.

The big question of course is this: what did I learn through the application of those key principles, theories and models used in the world of business to build high performing teams, in the world of sports.

Let's have a look at the next chapter.

Always do your best.

What you plant now you
will harvest later.

Og Mandino

Did it prove anything?

The "experiment" certainly proved or emphasised a number of things.

Firstly, the principles, theories and models used to build and maintain high performing teams in the workplace can be applied equally well in the world of sport, and bring about excellent results.

The principles of building high performance teams are exactly the same in both sectors; only the task being carried out by the team is different.

Secondly, the techniques and approaches for developing people and performance are exactly the same in both areas.

Development requires an understanding of the skills and knowledge required in order to deliver that which is needed to meet the performance criteria, a way of identifying the knowledge / skills gap, and an appropriate way of delivering the learning required.

Finally, the skills and techniques employed to motivate individuals and teams are the same.
Wherever people are being lead, the same motivational techniques can be applied, and

do work. High performance in both business and sport requires the creation of three things:

- Appropriate Knowledge Base.

    o Whatever individuals do, they need to have the knowledge appropriate to their required role. This is also true of leaders.

- Skills Base.

    o To succeed at a high level, individuals and teams need to have an appropriate level of skills to be able to carry out the task required of them.

- Motivation.

    o To perform at a high level requires the presence of a high level of motivation, as it is the driving force behind all action. High performance comes through a burning desire to achieve, and to do whatever it takes to do that.

Even with all these criteria in place, there is still one further requirement – ACTION.

Both leaders and those being lead are not worth much as long as they remain "technical experts." It is only the application of knowledge, through skills, that creates performance.

Ultimately, all success comes down to the effectiveness of the leader.

Effective leadership is about ensuring that the three requirements for high performance are all present in the right amounts, and that action results.

So what did the "Titans" achieve? The list is actually quite impressive, and includes:

1. From not being able to put together 12 players for early matches during the 2004 – 2005 season, the squad rose to 28, nearly enough for 2 teams. They finished the 2005-2006 season with 25, a net gain of over 13 players.

2. The squad played and defeated their contemporaries, getting to the semi-finals of the Under 13 Knock-Out Cup Competition.

3. We received over £3000.00 in sponsorship support from very kind

parents and businesses including GSK, manufacturers of Lucozade Sport.

4. The team received high praise and recognition from club coaches, opponent's coaches and referees.

5. We all learned a lot, and went on to become better as both players and coach.

6. We enjoyed ourselves and had fun, building a great team spirit and camaraderie amongst players, supporters and coach.

So what was learnt from this project? Let's see in the next chapter.

You see things and you
say "Why?"

But I dream of things
that never were and say
"Why Not?"

George Bernard Shaw

The Key Learning Points.

As far as I am concerned the project proved, beyond all reasonable doubt that the principles, theories and models used in business actually work, and, more than that could be used in the sporting world to do likewise.

One of the reasons I was delighted to have the opportunity to carry out this project with a rugby team was because I believe there are certain parallels between building a team in a business environment and doing the same in a rugby environment.

The reasons for that are:

Rugby is a very tough, physical game, and not for the faint hearted.

There is no hiding place on the rugby field – you have to do your job or you let the team down. It is the same in business, particularly with organisations running lean as they do these days.

The majority of the young players are more interested in the physical side of rugby, whether it be clattering others or trying to outrun them, than actually learning to play and the technical aspects that go with that.

That provides a certain level of challenge for the coach. This also includes the aspect of coaching safe practices which may conflict with advice being given in the home environment.

Managers and leaders in the workplace face challenges all the time – it goes with the territory.

If the experiment was to have worth, it had to deal with the same sort of issues.

Rugby is physically demanding and requires strength, fitness and stamina.

It can be played in some quite hostile environments, especially with regard to climatic conditions, so conditions are not always perfect.

One of the many reasons sometimes given by managers as the cause of poor performance in the workplace is the condition of the physical environment, and the challenge of replicating that was provided through this winter sport.

Finally, it is a competitive game, where performance and progress can be measured by results, therefore it is possible to monitor which direction things are going in.

In fact, it seems to me that it is just like the workplace.

The performance of a manager can be measured through performance indicators, in the same way that the performance of a rugby coach can be measured by results.

I felt it was a good parallel.

The project created an opportunity to identify, test and evaluate key principles and actions that were and are important to team success.

These are the areas that the leader, or coach, is, I believe, responsible for creating, facilitating or enabling through leadership action.

Without action by the leader, high performance teams do not develop.

Certainly a level of mediocrity may be achieved, but nothing else.

Leadership action in the three key areas has been identified as described in the following sections.

One who fears failure
limits his activities.
Failure is only the
opportunity to begin
again more intelligently.

Henry Ford

Motivation.

Overall, the key ingredient in success has to be the level of motivation present in the individual team members and the team itself.

It is this motivation that provides the energy needed to succeed at any level whether in sport or business.

People who feel good about themselves generally perform better and more consistently.

The role of the motivator is to make people feel good about themselves by making them feel special, valued.

Alongside this however is confidence.

Individuals have to feel confident in both themself and their abilities in order to be effective.

The role of the leader is undeniably to create the right environment or climate that will generate and inspire motivation because then the leader has something to harness and channel.

I have sadly seen experience rugby players turned coaches gradually destroy their squads, ending up with insufficient players to put teams together simply because they have failed to effectively motivate their teams.

All the technical knowledge in the world is of little use if you have no-one to impart it to.

I have seen exactly the same thing occur in business leaders as well, where they have ignored or avoided issues concerning personal motivation.

Technical knowledge and expertise is very important, but can be obtained from a range of sources.

However it is the human spirit that delivers, and that process needs to be actively managed.

Without motivation nothing happens. The most powerful motivation of all is self motivation, and leadership is about enabling self motivation to occur. Self motivation is about achievement, about gain, and people generally can find a way to get what they really want.

The other major type of motivation is really concerned with avoidance, usually of something unpleasant.

Whilst it can be a very powerful motivator in the short term, in the long term it has limited use.

Leaders should focus on building high levels of self motivation and the following can and will contribute to this:

- Find opportunities to provide recognition and praise, no matter how small. Make sure it is sincere and genuine, and use it to leverage performance upwards.

- If necessary, create opportunities through which individuals can achieve, in order to be able to provide recognition.

- Ensure the right / appropriate level of challenge is created, to make achieving meaningful.

- Take a personal interest in the individual, finding out about them and their aspirations, then help them to realise them.

- Enable individual success, within the team taking into account levels of ability.

- Set high expectations for individuals and the team, and encourage both to meet them.

- Create a positive vision for the team performance and encourage people to strive for its attainment.

- In difficult times remind individuals of past successes and achievements, creating a positive outlook and rebuilding enthusiasm.

- Be approachable, and sensitive to their needs – discounting and dismissal should be avoided at all costs.

- Encourage individuals to build pride in themselves and their team.

- Find ways to recognise and acknowledge everyone's contribution, no matter how small or insignificant it may seem in the great scheme of things.

- Manage the expectations of the individuals to avoid disappointment and a drop in motivation

To live is not merely to breathe – it is to act.

Michelangelo

Teamwork

High performance teams do not come about by accident. They have to be created, built.

The role of the leader is to turn individuals into high performing individuals, and groups into high performing teams.

People naturally turn themselves into a group, but generally do not have the knowledge or skills to go the extra mile to become a team.

Leaders need to facilitate this transition.

The following actions can and will assist this:

- Encourage teamwork and a co-operative approach at all times.

- Stamp out individualism where it is seen as competing with team effectiveness.

- Reward team performance through praise and recognition.

- Involve everyone in the creation of team success.

- If the team can deal with internal friction, conflict and its own underperformance itself let it; otherwise teach them how to do it.

- Defend the weak and temporarily disadvantaged / despondent until their strength returns – people develop and recover at differing rates.

- Recognise the team will unite together against the leader from time to time – manage it don't "flatten" it – sometimes leaders are wrong!

- Maintain the balance within the team, preventing bullying etc. Everyone is entitled to get their own needs met, and to be treated equally and fairly.

- Work to create a team role for everyone as quickly as possible, so they know where they fit into the team and how they contribute.

- Find ways to recognise and acknowledge everyone's contribution, no matter how small or insignificant it may seem in the great scheme of things.

- Hand over responsibility to the team for self managing as soon as it is practicable.

- Help facilitate the creation of a team identity, separate to the official identity to which the team members can commit their loyalty.

- Work hard to create high levels of team spirit, the backbone of the team environment.

Leadership

Leadership is about making things happen, particularly those things which lead to high performance.

Leadership is built around three things, being direction, motivation and assertiveness.

Direction is about providing a focus for team activities – it sets out the results the team seek to achieve and the quality and quantity standards by which success are measured.

Motivation includes facilitating individual and team motivation, and creating the climate and team environment in which motivation can be inspired and flourish.

Assertiveness is about dealing with any internal or external issues that can impact negatively on an individual's or the team's performance, and reduce the effectiveness of either or both.

To be effective at leadership, leaders and coaches need to:

- Work at it all the time, as leadership is continuous.

*To become what we are
capable of becoming is the
only end in life.*

Robert Louis Stevenson

- Be aware of and seek opportunities to exert leadership influence in a robust and positive manner.

- Be a leader, and not just "do" leadership.

- Look for and create opportunities to deliver effective leadership.

- Deal with issues in an effective and timely manner, rather then ignoring them or hoping they will either go away or improve of their own accord.

- Seek opportunities to motivate individuals and the team in a positive manner.

- Do whatever has to be done, and don't seek shortcuts.

- Be prepared to undo existing success to succeed at a higher level.

- Work with whatever mess they create.

- Work with what is available, and not wish for something better unless prepared to go out and make it happen.

- Recognise nothing happens by chance on a regular and consistent basis.

- Realise that leadership can be uncomfortable as you have to deal with issues and resolve them in a satisfactory manner.

- Understand that leaders are made not born.

- Leadership is easy, if you do the right things right!

- Anyone can be a leader although some may have to work harder at it and success may take a little longer.

- Realise that sometimes you have to go backwards to go forwards.

- Understand that very often, the little things can make a big difference.

Leaders need to believe in themselves and their own abilities.

They also have to believe in their ability to learn what needs to be learned. This includes listening to the views and ideas of others without necessarily accepting them as being correct or more valid than their own.

Above all else, leadership is about action – about doing things, the right things, to create high performing teams capable of producing results.

There is only one true
success in life – to live
your life in your own
way.

Christopher Morley

In Conclusion.

When this "project" started I was interested to see if the methods used in the corporate environment could be used to great effect in the world of sports, namely on the rugby field.

I wanted to know if the principles, models and theories from the world of business could be applied in a sports environment and if so to what success. .

Having had the opportunity, I can say with confidence that the methods used in the world of business can be applied very successfully in a sports environment, and vice versa, because a high performing team is just that, whether in business or sport.

The only significant difference lies in what the team does - what it delivers – the technical component.

Is either more important than the other? Yes, I think so.

If you can build the team side of things, you can hold the team together whilst the skills and knowledge bases are being built, but all the technical knowledge in the world will not be any use if the team is not created.

Again there are parallels in both business and sport.

In business, technically expert individuals are put in charge of "teams" because of their "expert knowledge" only to find performance is poor.

Similarly in sport, ex-players, even those who played at a high level, become coaches, based on their experience and reputation, only for some of them to have difficulty in creating successful teams.

Successful teams need to be created, inspired and motivated.

They also need to be provided with the technical components as well if they are to go on to perform at the highest levels.

Motivation is without a doubt the key to everything in life.

As a coach or manager take time to get to know your people, and find out what really makes them tick. If you can find a way to help them, do whatever it takes to do so.

Help them develop a positive and healthy self esteem, and a positive self image.

Provide them with genuine and sincere praise for a job well done and they will stay loyal to you.

Always remember, it is never enough simply to know – success comes through what you do.

Therefore always make the effort to do the right things, do them well and do them often.

Above all, be yourself and enjoy what you do. If you are not motivated it will show, and then for you everything is lost.

Make the time to refresh and renew your belief in yourself, then use it to help others develop and grow.

I hope that in some small way the contents of this book will inspire and motivate you to follow your dreams, whatever they are, whatever they mean to you.

I hope it will help you to go on to develop your leadership effectiveness. You in turn can then go on to help people to develop themselves and achieve what lies within them, inspiring their motivation, harnessing their energy and harvesting their potential.

Good Luck!

The Man Who Thinks He Can!

If you think you are beaten, you are;
If you think you dare not, you don't!
If you'd like to win, but think you can't,
It's almost a cinch that you wont.

If you think you'll lose, you're lost
For out in the world we find
Success begins with a fellow's will;
It's all in the state of mind!

If you think you're outclassed, you are;
You've got to think high to rise.
You've got to be sure of yourself
before you can win the prize.

Life's battles don't always go
To the strongest or fastest man;
But sooner or later the man who wins
Is the man who thinks he can!

Walter D. Wintle

NOTES:

Recommended Reading List.

A selection of books you may care to choose from.

BUSINESS / PERSONAL DEVELOPMENT:

Alpha Plan - David Lewis
Asserting Yourself - Lineham & Egan
Assertiveness At Work - D R Stubbs
Awaken The Giant Within - Tony Robbins
Body Language - Alan Pease
Body Language - Dr Joseph Braysich
Born To Win - James And Jongeward
Changing The Game - Larry Wilson
Effective Performance Appraisals - R B Maddox
Effective Problem Solving - Dave Francis
Effective Teambuilding - John Adair
Effective Time Management - John Adair
Games People Play - Eric Berne
Getting To Yes - Fisher & Ury
Going For It - Victor Kiam
How To Be An Even Better Manager – 1 + 2 - Michael Armstrong
How To Develop Your Personal Management Skills - June Allan
I Can - Ben Sweetland
I'm O.K. - You're O.K. - Thomas and Amy Harris
Introducing Neuro-Linguistic Programming- O'Connor &
Seymour
Journey Of Awakening - Ram Dass
Leadership And The One Minute Manager - Blanchard, Zigami
And Zigami
Leadership Skills For Women - Manning And Haddock
Live Your Dreams - Les Brown
Magic Of Thinking Big - David J. Schwartz
Magic Of Thinking Success -   "   "
Making The Most Of Your Mind - Tony Buzan
Man's Search For Meaning - Victor Frankl
Management Teams - Why The Succeed Or Fail - Meredith Belbin
Managing Negotiations - Kennedy, Benson And McMillan
Maximum Personal Energy - Knutzleman
Mindmapping - Joyce Wycoff
Not Bosses But Leaders - John Adair
One Minute Manager Builds High Performance Teams - Blanchard
And Parisi - Carew
Positive Workaholism - Dennis Hensley
Psycho - Cybernetics - Maxwell Maltz
Pulling Your Own Strings - W Dyer
Relax: Dealing With Stress - Watts & Cooper
Self Managing Teams - R Hicks And D Bone
Staying Ahead Of Time - Dennis Hensley
Staying O.K. - Amy & Thomas Harris

Stress For Success - Dr Peter Hanson
Success Through A Positive Mental Attitude - Hill & Stone
Successful Negotiators Handbook - David Farmer
Super Confidence - Gael Lindenfield
T A Today - Ian Stewart And Vann Joines
Tactics - Edward De Bono
Talk It Out - Daniel Dana
Teamroles At Work - M Belbin
The 10 Day Relaxation Plan - Dr Eric Trimmer
The Art Of War - Sun Tzu
The Creative Manager - Roger Evans & Peter Russel
 The Hidden Advantage In Selling - Donald J. Moine & John H.
Herd
The Joy Of Stress -   "   "
The One Minute Manager - Blanchard And Johnson
The One Minute Manager Meets The Monkey - Blanchard And
Lorber
The Psychology Of Interpersonal Behaviour - Michael Argyle
The Steps To Self Development - Tom Jaap
The Success System That Never Fails - W. Clement Stone
The Tao Of Leadership - John Heider
The Tao of Coaching – Max Lansberg
Effective Coaching – Marshall J Cook
The Tao Of Management - Bob Messing
The Tao Of Peace - Diane Dreher
Think And Grow Rich - Napoleon Hill
Time Trap - Alec Mc Kenzie
Understanding Organisations - Charles Handy
Unlimited Power - Anthony Robbins
Use Your Head - Tony Buzan
What Do You Say After You Say Hello? - Eric Berne
What Do You Say When You Talk To Yourself - Shad Helmstetter

RUGBY:

Total Rugby – Jim Greenwood
Think Rugby – Jim Greenwood
Rugby Union – Peter Johnson
Heading for the Top – Kerry Wedd
Rugby – A Players Guide to the Laws – Derek Robinson
SAQ Rugby – Alan Pearson
Rugby – Steps to Success – Tony Briscombe and Peter Drewett

Printed in the United Kingdom
by Lightning Source UK Ltd.
132095UK00001B/180/A